ROCK EXPLORER

FOSSILS

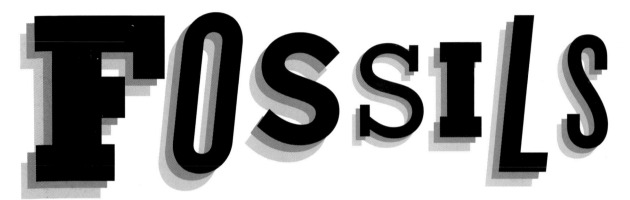

Claudia Martin

D0276009

Quarto is the authority on a wide range of topics.

Quarto educates, entertains and enriches the lives of our readers—enthusiasts and lovers of hands-on living.

www.quartoknows.com

Editor: Clare Hibbert
Designer: Dave Ball

© 2018 Quarto Publishing plc
Text © Claudia Martin

First Published in 2017 by QED Publishing,
an imprint of The Quarto Group.
The Old Brewery, 6 Blundell Street,
London N7 9BH, United Kingdom.
T (0)20 7700 6700 F (0)20 7700 8066
www.QuartoKnows.com

All rights reserved. No part of this publication may be reproduced, stored in a retrieval system, or transmitted in any form or by any means, electronic, mechanical, photocopying, recording, or otherwise, without the prior permission of the publisher, nor be otherwise circulated in any form of binding or cover other than that in which it is published and without a similar condition being imposed on the subsequent purchaser.

A catalogue record for this book is available from the British Library.

ISBN 978-1-78493-966-3

Manufactured in Guangdong, China TT022018

9 8 7 6 5 4 3 2 1

MIX
Paper from responsible sources
FSC® C016973

LEWISHAM LIBRARY SERVICE	
Askews & Holts	03-Apr-2018
J560 JUNIOR NON-FICT	15

Contents

What is a Fossil?

Fossils are the remains of animals and plants that lived thousands or millions of years ago.

FOUND IN ROCKS

Fossils are usually found in rocks. Palaeontologists are scientists who dig up fossils – very carefully!

Palaeontologists find and study fossils.

LOOK INTO THE PAST

Over millions of years, Earth's animals and plants have slowly changed. Fossils show us what animals and plants looked like long ago.

Without fossils, we would not know that dinosaurs existed! ▼

Oldest fossils

Incredibly small tubes of bacteria preserved in rocks in Canada date back 4.2 billion years. They show us the first life forms on Earth.

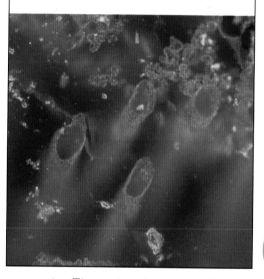

▲ These bacteria are the oldest-known fossils.

How Fossils
Form

Most animals and plants rot away after they die. Luckily, when something dies in a suitable spot, a fossil can form.

BODY FOSSILS

A body fossil is the remains of an animal's body or a plant. It can form when the remains are buried in sand or mud. Over time, the sand or mud turn to stone – and so do any hard parts of the animal or plant, such as bones, shells, teeth or bark.

Dragon bones?

For thousands of years, people found dinosaur fossils but did not know what they were. The ancient Chinese thought they were dragon bones.

This body fossil is *Pterodactylus*, a flying reptile that lived 150 million years ago.

TRACE FOSSILS

A trace fossil is not a plant or animal's body. It is a mark or trace left by a living thing. Trace fossils include footprints, burrows and poo!

This fossilized dinosaur poo has hardened into rock.

Hunting for
Fossils

Anyone can go looking for fossils.
Where are the best places to look?

FOSSIL HOTSPOTS
You often find fossils in
sedimentary rock, such
as sandstone and chalk.
These rocks formed from
layers of sand or mud.

▲ These sandstone cliffs in
England contain fossils from
around 200 million years ago.

This dinosaur skull was found ▶
in sandstone in Utah, USA.

JIGSAW PUZZLE

When a palaeontologist finds a fossil, they cut it carefully out of the rock. Back at the laboratory, they clean it and piece together broken parts.

◄ A palaeontologist cleans a *Triceratops*'s horn.

Get a move on!

Palaeontologists examine bones for signs of how they were attached to muscles. This gives clues about how the animal moved.

Reconstruction ► of a *T. rex*'s leg

Sea **Creatures**

Life on Earth began in the sea. Some of the oldest fossils we have found are of sea creatures.

AMAZING AMMONITES

Ammonites looked like squid inside spiral-shaped shells.

Ammonites are one of the easiest fossils to find. ▶

TOP TRILOBITES

Trilobites were soft-bodied creatures with a hard covering, like a crab.

▲ Trilobites looked a bit like woodlice.

DOLPHIN-SHAPED

Icthyosaurs were
swimming reptiles.
They had streamlined
bodies, like dolphins.

Icthyosaurs
lived from
250 to
90 million
years ago.

FISH FOSSILS

The first fish appeared
530 million years ago.

This spiny fish lived
40 million years ago.

Living fossil

People thought the coelacanth
(say 'see-lo-canth') fish died
out with the dinosaurs. Then, in
1938, live ones were discovered!

Discovering
Dinosaurs

The dinosaurs were an amazing group of reptiles. They first walked the Earth 230 million years ago.

The sauropods were huge plant-eating dinosaurs with long necks.

FUNNY WALK

Like other reptiles, dinosaurs breathed air, had leathery skins and laid eggs. Unlike other reptiles, dinosaurs walked with their legs straight under their bodies, not sprawled out to the sides.

Fossilized dinosaur skin

Dinosaur tracks in Colorado, USA

DIFFERENT DIETS

Some dinosaurs were hunters who ate other dinosaurs and animals for food. Others fed on plants.

Meat-eating *T. rex*'s teeth were around 30 cm long.

Terrible lizards

Dinosaur means 'terrible lizard' in Greek. The biggest meat-eaters, such as Allosaurus (below), had huge, powerful jaws.

This fossilized egg is from *Hadrosaurus*, a plant-eating dinosaur.

Strange and **Extinct**

Dinosaurs are not the only strange animals that once roamed the Earth. Fossils have taught us about others.

EARLY ELEPHANTS

Mammoths had trunks and were related to today's elephants. They died out 4,500 years ago.

Mammoth skeleton ▶

SLIMY LIZARD

Seymouria looked like a lizard, but it was an amphibian, like a frog. It lived in water when young, then crawled onto land as an adult.

▲ *Seymouria* lived 280 million years ago.

CURVED BLADES

Smilodon's nickname is the sabre-toothed tiger, and it is easy to see why. It died out 11,000 years ago.

▲ *Smilodon*'s name means 'knife tooth'. Its curved canines were 30 cm long.

Sabre-toothed squirrel

Some fossils are really weird! One fossil from Argentina is of a squirrel-like creature with long, sharp teeth.

Wonderful
Wings

When did animals first flap through the air? Fossils can give us the answer!

FLUTTERING INSECTS

Insects were the earliest flying animals. The oldest fossils of winged insects are 400 million years old.

Millions of years ago, this gnat got stuck in resin that oozed from a tree. The resin slowly hardened into stone called amber.

Dragonflies have been darting about for 325 million years.

WINGED DINOSAURS

Over millions of years, dinosaurs evolved (changed). By 150 million years ago, some dinosaurs had wings.

Alive and well

Most dinosaurs died
out 66 million years ago,
possibly after an asteroid
hit Earth. Only the winged
dinosaurs survived. Today,
we call them birds.

Archaeopteryx
was one of the
first winged
dinosaurs. This
fossil shows
traces of its
feathers.

Precious
Plants

Some of the most beautiful fossils are plants. Look out for fossilized leaves, stems, trunks and even petals.

COMPLETELY PETRIFIED

Petrified means 'turned to rock'. Wood can turn to rock when it is buried under sand or mud. Over time, minerals grow in the wood, replacing its living material with rock.

Petrified tree stumps in Arizona, USA

LOVELY LEAVES

Cycads are plants with large, stiff leaves. Fossils tell us that they have hardly changed in the last 150 million years.

◄ Fossilized cycad leaves

Today cycads usually grow in hot countries. ►

FAINT FLOWER

Fossilized flowers are very rare because petals are so delicate.

◄ This flower fossil is 35 million years old.

Watch your step!

The nearest fossil may be closer than you think. Look down! Paving stones can contain fossilized ferns.

Our **Family**

Modern humans evolved 200,000 years ago. What did humans look like before they looked like you?

APELIKE ANCESTOR

Humans evolved from creatures called hominins. One of the most famous hominin fossils, 'Lucy', lived 3.2 million years ago.

This cast of Lucy's skull shows that her brain was small, like an ape's.

Lucy walked upright, like a modern human. She probably slept in tree nests at night, like an ape.

FOSSILIZED FOOTPRINTS

Ancient tracks tell us when hominins began walking upright on two legs.

◄ Upright-walking hominins left these footprints in Tanzania, Africa, 3.7 million years ago.

Close competitors

Neanderthals were close cousins of modern humans. They died out around 40,000 years ago.

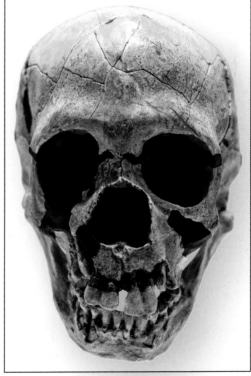

Fossil
Guide

AMBER
Description: Hardened tree resin that can contain minibeasts
Where to find: Fairly common in rocks or on beaches

AMMONITE
Description: Spiral shell (or a mould of the shell's insides)
Where to find: Fairly common on cliffs and beaches

COPROLITE
Description: Animal poo
Where to find: Very rare, in rocks worldwide

DINOSAUR
Description: Bones, teeth, eggs or marks left by skin or feathers
Where to find: Rare, in deserts and cliffs

FOOTPRINT
Description: The shape of an animal's foot, pressed into mud
Where to find: Rare, where rock is worn away by waves or cut away by mining or construction

HOMININ
Description: Bones, teeth or footprints of early humans or humanlike creatures
Where to find: Very rare, with the oldest examples found in Africa

MAMMOTH
Description: Bones, tusks and teeth of elephantlike animals
Where to find: Rare, in Africa, Asia, Europe and North America

PETRIFIED WOOD
Description: Wood that has turned to rock
Where to find: Fairly common worldwide, below and above ground

TRILOBITE
Description: Body parts of shelled sea creatures (or a mould of their shape)
Where to find: Common fossil in cliffs and quarries